YO-YO
TRICKS

"Fast" Eddy McDonald is a three-time Guinness World Record Holder. He holds the records for: most Loop the Loop in one hour (8437); most Loop the Loop in three hours (21,663); and most tricks in one minute where the yo-yo must return to the hand after each trick (35).

YO-YO
TRICKS

By "Fast" Eddy McDonald

This edition published in 2020
By SpiceBox™
12171 Horseshoe Way,
Richmond, BC,
Canada V7A 4V4

First published in 2009
© SpiceBox™ 2009

ISBN 13: 978-1-926567-17-4

CEO and Publisher: Ben Lotfi
Author: Edward McDonald
Editor: AnnMarie MacKinnon
Creative Director: Garett Chan
Art Director: Christine Covert
Designer: Morgen Matheson
Production: James Badger, Mell D'Clute
Sourcing: Tony Su, Carman Fung

For more SpiceBox products and information, visit our website:
www.spiceboxbooks.com

Manufactured in China

13 15 17 19 20 18 16 14

TABLE OF CONTENTS

How did "Fast" Eddy get so good? He practices—all the time! He began his yo-yo career at 12 and practiced so much, he was touring the world by the age of 16.

INTRODUCTION
Welcome to The World of Yo-Yos

The world of yo-yos is an amazing place. The yo-yo has a very long and interesting history, and can be found in almost every country around the world.

The great thing about yo-yos is that you can do so many amazing tricks with a toy that fits right in your pocket. And it's pretty easy to learn. You'll be able to do basic yo-yo tricks in a short period of time and more advanced tricks with a bit of practice. Some of the more incredible tricks, such as the Coin trick or the Haircut can take a lifetime to master. There are thousands of established yo-yo tricks to learn and new ones are being invented every day. Invent your own yo-yo tricks and be sure to give them a great name!

In this book, we have assembled everything you'll need along your path to becoming a yo-yo expert. The yo-yo tricks, instructions and gear included in this kit are all you need to learn the art of yo-yo playing. To make learning all the tricks a little easier, it's important to learn the tricks in the order they appear in the book. Each one you learn will help you prepare for the next trick in this book. Most importantly, don't forget to practice, practice, and then practice a little bit more. Yo for it!

THE HISTORY OF THE YO-YO

We sometimes think of yo-yos as a relatively recent North American invention, but they've been around for a very long time, and have been a popular toy around the world. While it's not entirely clear where the yo-yo originated, it made its first recorded appearance around 500 B.C. on a plate from Greece.

The plate shows a drawing of a young boy playing with what appears to be a yo-yo. The yo-yo also appears among British and French aristocrats in the late 1700s and early 1800s. At that time the yo-yo was called a bandalore and was often sterling silver. The word yo-yo comes from the native Philippine language of

Over time the yo-yo has had several other names such as "spinner", "return top", "rollin", "jo-jo" and "quiz".

Tagalog, and translates to *come-come* in English. The yo-yo has a very long history in the Philippines. It is believed that the yo-yo was originally used as a weapon for hunting. The hunter would hide in a tree and throw a large chunk of wood or rock with a long thick cord attached, in an attempt to catch his prey.

The yo-yo was first seen in North America in the early 1900s when yo-yo experts from the Philippines arrived and trained players from across North America in the art. Around this same time, the yo-yo string was looped around the axle for the first time allowing the yo-yo to spin or sleep at the bottom. This opened the door to the endless trick possibilities that continue today.

ALL ABOUT YOUR YO-YO

Yo-yos are generally made from three different kinds of materials: wood, plastic, or metal. Each has its advantages and disadvantages. Wood is classic, durable, and timeless. Plastic is the material most often used to make yo-yos. It's tough and easily moldable. Metal yo-yos are generally made from aluminum and are much heavier than wood or plastic yo-yos.

The biggest consideration when choosing the right yo-yo for you is the type of axle.

Different Kinds of Yo-Yos

Originally, yo-yos were carved from a solid piece of wood, and this is where the **fixed axle yo-yo** comes from. Fixed axle yo-yos have an unmoving axle joining the two halves of the yo-yo. This is the simplest and most "old school" type of yo-yo.

TIP: Make sure you change your string often. It will make your tricks flow much more smoothly.

Transaxle yo-yos have a fixed axle, but also have the addition of a sleeve that goes around the fixed axle. This sleeve reduces friction and lets the yo-yo spin for much longer than a traditional yo-yo.

The **ball bearing yo-yo** is similar to a transaxle yo-yo, but instead of a simple sleeve, the sleeve is actually filled with metal balls that further reduce the friction of the spinning yo-yo.

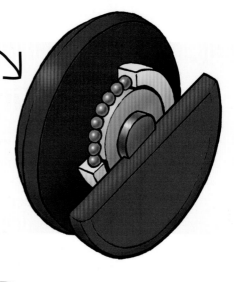

The **clutch yo-yo** is the one commonly selected by beginners because it always returns to your hand. The fast spinning motion of the yo-yo keeps the "clutch" open. Once the yo-yo begins to slow down, the clutch snaps shut and it returns to your hand.

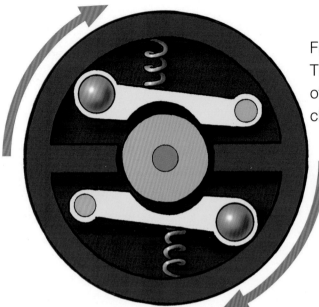

Fig. 1:
The spinning motion of the yo-yo keeps the clutch open.

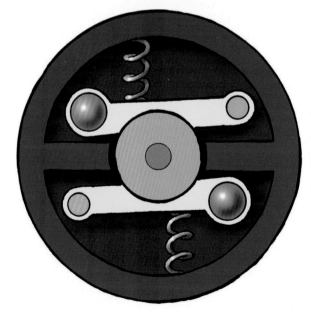

Fig. 2:
When the spinning of the yo-yo slows, the clutch grabs the axle, causing the yo-yo to return to your hand.

What Yo-Yo Should I Use?

There are several different kinds of yo-yos, and the one that you choose to play with will depend on your skill level and what tricks you will be doing.

A beginner yo-yo will return to your hand automatically. As the Sleeper slows down, the yo-yo slows down, activating the centrifugal clutch (as in Fig. 1). The clutch will grab the yo-yo's axle and the yo-yo winds up returning to your hand (as in Fig. 2). The downfall of this yo-yo is that the Sleeper is not very long and it can return when you don't want it to.

The transaxle yo-yo, or bearing yo-yo, is meant for extreme Sleepers. This yo-yo has a bearing system or sleeve over the fixed axle allowing for very long Sleepers. Some bearing yo-yos can sleep for 10 minutes and still return to your hand. The down side is that not all tricks require the Sleeper and this yo-yo is difficult to prevent from sleeping.

The traditional yo-yo, or fixed axle yo-yo, is the best all around yo-yo and the most difficult to use. This yo-yo does not have a bearing or a clutch. The string is looped directly around its axle. The traditional yo-yo can be adjusted to do both tricks that require the Sleeper and tricks that don't by changing how tight the yo-yo string is around the axle. Turn the yo-yo to the right to tighten and the left to loosen.

"Fast" Eddy says:

"You can learn how to do almost anything with hard work and practice! Yo for it!"

15

Winding Up Your Yo-Yo String

Let the yo-yo hang down, hold the yo-yo with your free hand. Wrap the string around the yo-yo until it's completely wound up. If the string is very loose around the axle you will need to do this very slowly in order to get the yo-yo to catch around the axle and begin to wind up.

Here is another way to wind up your yo-yo that's a little harder to master. Start by letting the yo-yo hang down, and with your free hand hold the yo-yo down with some force, pulling the string tight. With your thumb in the groove of the yo-yo push down with force in an attempt to get the yo-yo spinning. If this is done correctly the yo-yo will wind up into your hand.

Changing Your String

To keep your yo-yo in good working order, it's best to change your string often to avoid having it break. When changing your yo-yo string, also use string that is meant specifically for yo-yos. A real yo-yo string has a loop at one end that goes around your yo-yo. In fact a yo-yo string is a single string that has been doubled, tied at the top and twisted. There is only a knot at the end of the string that attaches to your finger.

How Long Should My String Be?

Your yo-yo string should run from your waist to the floor while the string is attached to the yo-yo. If the yo-yo string is too long, cut the string (or have an adult do it) six centimeters (two inches) above your waist and make a loop in the string. Now pull the string through the loop making a slipknot. Place the slipknot on your middle finger between your first and second knuckle.

This is the best place to attach your yo-yo string to your hand. Now you're ready to yo!

17

CHANGE YOUR STRING ON A...

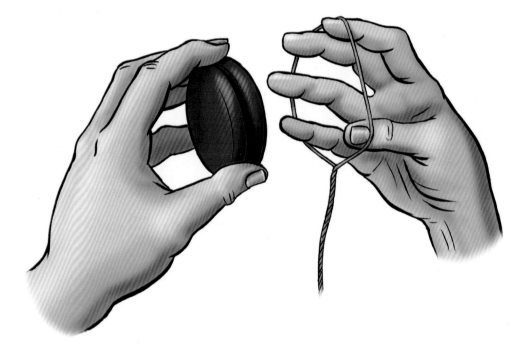

...Fixed Axle Yo-Yo

The string on a fixed axle yo-yo is looped around the axle, not tied to the axle. The axle is actually spinning inside the string.

The first step is to remove all the string from inside the yo-yo. If you have some string left inside the yo-yo it needs to be removed. Most fixed axle yo-yos do not come apart. You will need to use a paper clip or a nail file to pick the string out of the yo-yo. Then you're ready to change your string. Take the looped end of the new string and untwist it or open it up to allow the yo-yo to slip inside the string. Now let the string go and it will twist back up.

...Transaxle Yo-Yo

The string on a transaxle yo-yo is looped around the bearing or the transaxle that is on the main axle. In a transaxle yo-yo, the loop is doubled to help the yo-yo respond better.

Most transaxle yo-yos have the ability to come apart. This makes removing and attaching new string easier. As with a fixed axle yo-yo, all old string must be removed from the inside of the yo-yo.

Take the looped end of the new string and untwist it or open it up to allow the yo-yo to slip inside the string. Now twist the string once and loop it over the yo-yo again. Let the string go and it will twist back up.

Now you're ready to yo!!!

THE TEN
BASIC
TRICKS

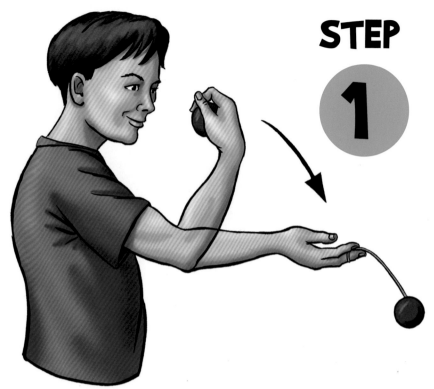

The Sleeper

This is the most important trick because it's the basis for so many other tricks. After the yo-yo is attached to your finger (for tips see page 17), place it in your hand with your palm facing up and the string under the yo-yo. Position your arm as if you were making a muscle with your bicep. Now throw the yo-yo, with medium strength towards the ground extending your arm. It's more of a cast out and down rather than a throw directly to the ground. The yo-yo should make a small arc on its way down. When the yo-yo reaches the bottom of the string it will spin, without returning to your hand. That's the Sleeper.

STEP

2

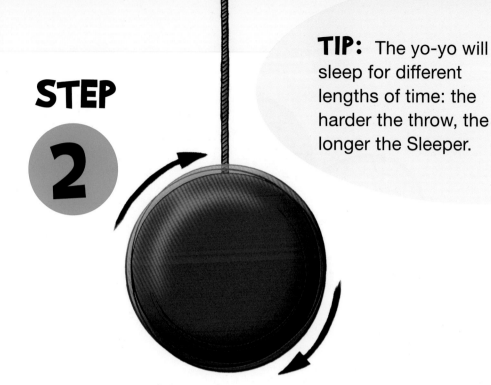

TIP: The yo-yo will sleep for different lengths of time: the harder the throw, the longer the Sleeper.

Turn your hand palm down. A quick jerk upward should be all you need to make the yo-yo return. The yo-yo will need to have enough spin left to wind back up into your hand and you'll need to watch it on its way back up so that you'll be ready to catch it. The yo-yo won't sleep if there are knots in your string. Be sure to check the string around the axle for knots. If the string is too tight or very old the yo-yo will not sleep. (See Changing Your String, page 17.) Practice this trick until you can do it really well. The first step in the next trick is to do the Sleeper.

The Sleeper will take different amounts of time to learn for different people so don't give up. Practice, practice, then practice a little bit more.

Burp The Baby

First, throw a medium strength Sleeper. As soon as the yo-yo sleeps at the bottom of the string announce the trick: "Here is Burp The Baby!" Place your free hand above your yo-yo hand, which should be facing palm down. As you jerk the yo-yo string up to return the yo-yo to your hand, pat the back of your yo-yo hand with your free hand, simulating burping a baby. Catch the yo-yo.

TIP: If your Sleeper is not long enough to accomplish this trick, try throwing your yo-yo a little harder.

STEP 1

Walk the Dog

This is one of the most popular yo-yo tricks around. To do a good Walk the Dog you will first need to throw the longest Sleeper you can. The longer the yo-yo sleeps, the longer that you can Walk the Dog. When the yo-yo sleeps at the bottom of the string you need to gently touch the yo-yo to the ground. The natural spin of the yo-yo

will pull it forward along the ground. Just before the yo-yo begins to slow down, jerk upward on the string. This will cause the yo-yo to return to your hand. It really looks like you are walking the dog.

STEP 1

The Forward Pass

This is the first trick in which you don't throw the yo-yo down. Instead you will throw it forward. Start with your arm hanging down at your side. The back of your hand should be facing forward.

TIP: This trick will be easier if your string is tight. Let your yo-yo hang down at the end of its string. Turn the yo-yo several times to the right to tighten it.

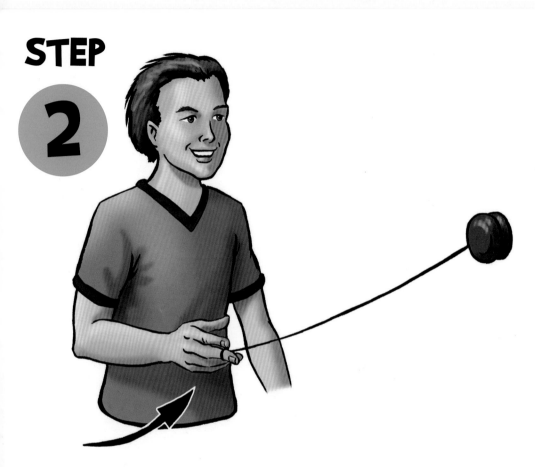

Swing your arm back and then forward releasing the yo-yo with medium force just as your arm passes your hip. Aim your yo-yo straight ahead and extend your arm straight out. After you release the yo-yo, turn your hand over so that your palm is up. Keep your eye on the yo-yo and prepare to catch. If the yo-yo is not returning to your hand try throwing it a bit harder.

To complete any trick the yo-yo must return to your hand. If you cannot do this trick three times in a row perfectly, do not move on to the next trick.

STEP

1

TIP: Make sure the area you're doing the trick in is clear of any obstructions. It's best to do this trick outside in a wide open area.

Around The World

The goal of Around the World is for the yo-yo to make a complete circle and return to your hand. As in the last trick (the Forward Pass), start with your arm hanging down at your side. The back of your hand should be facing forward. This time, take your arm farther backwards and then forward. Remember, the harder the throw the longer the yo-yo will sleep. This time the yo-yo needs to be released towards the ground. Releasing the yo-yo towards the ground allows the yo-yo to sleep.

Guide the yo-yo with your hand, turning the wrist to make the yo-yo complete the circle. When the yo-yo completes the circle a quick jerk of the string will cause the yo-yo to return to your hand.

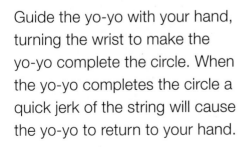

The Breakaway

In this trick, the yo-yo will be thrown to the side. The object is to have the yo-yo make a half circle across the front of your body (and, of course, return to your hand)!

STEP

1

STEP

2

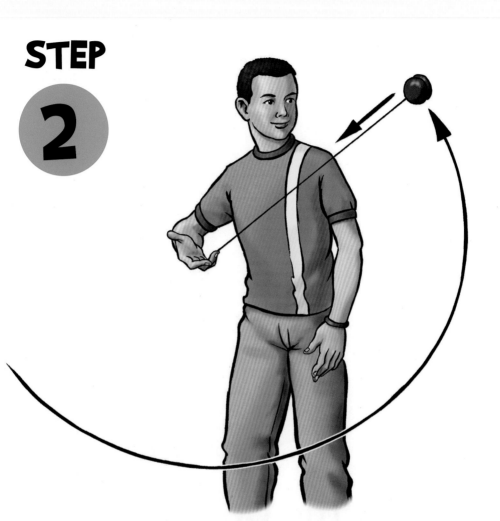

Start by bending your arm up at your side as if you're making a muscle. With your palm facing out throw your yo-yo in an outward casting motion causing the yo-yo to sleep. You need to use extra force when throwing the yo-yo for this trick. Now guide the yo-yo across your body using your lower arm and wrist. After the yo-yo crosses your body, a quick jerk of the string will cause the yo-yo to return to your hand.

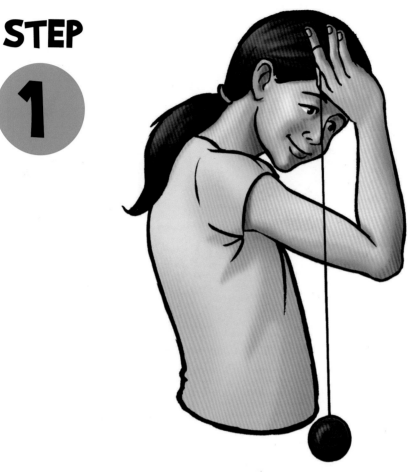

Around The Corner

The object of this trick is to have the yo-yo come over your shoulder, go down, then return to your hand so you'll need a good Sleeper to pull it off. Begin with a good Sleeper. Then extend your arm straight in front of you. This will allow room for you to twist your arm with the yo-yo still sleeping and move the yo-yo around your side and behind your back!

A quick jerk of the string will cause the yo-yo to return over your shoulder and down to the ground in front of you. If the Sleeper is long enough the yo-yo will then return to your hand.

TIP: A new string is a good way to get a longer Sleeper. Change your string often.

The Creeper

The object of this trick is for the yo-yo to creep back to your hand while your hand is on the ground. It looks great when it's done correctly. First throw a medium strength Sleeper. Next, swing the sleeping yo-yo forwards to its farthest point, keeping the yo-yo six inches off the ground. When the yo-yo gets to its farthest point away from you, allow your yo-yo to lightly touch the ground as in Walk the Dog. Crouch down and touch your hand to the ground

STEP

2

TIP: Make sure your string is the correct length for you. If your string is too long, this trick will be much more difficult.

when your yo-yo reaches its farthest point of Walk the Dog. Your hand should touch the ground at about the same time. Otherwise the trick won't work. After your hand touches the ground, a quick jerk of the string will cause the yo-yo to return to your hand along the ground. Keep your palm facing up so that you can catch the yo-yo.

Rock The Baby

This classic trick is almost as famous as the yo-yo itself. It will require a long Sleeper, so throw your yo-yo hard. The object of this trick is to create a triangle from the yo-yo string, known as the "cradle", and rock the yo-yo "baby" through it. The first step is to learn how to make the cradle. The best way to get good at making the cradle is to practice without the yo-yo spinning. Start by hanging the yo-yo down. Now move your free hand half way down in front of the string. With your palm facing down, pinch the string. Take your

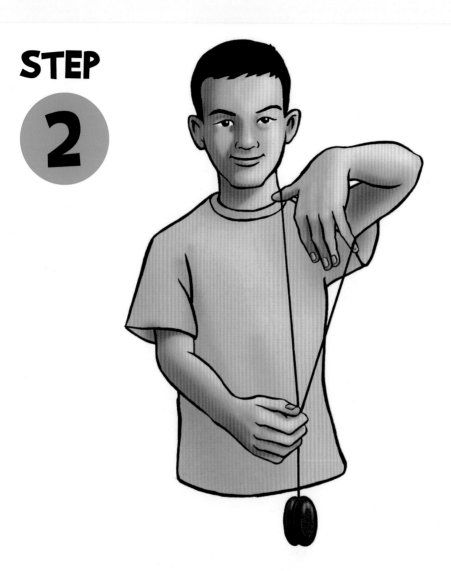

yo-yo hand and move it over the hand that is half way down the string, basically folding the string almost in half. Now pinch the string again. This will make the top of the cradle. Now turn the cradle over so that the triangle is upright.

If you have made the cradle/triangle the right size the yo-yo will now

STEP

3

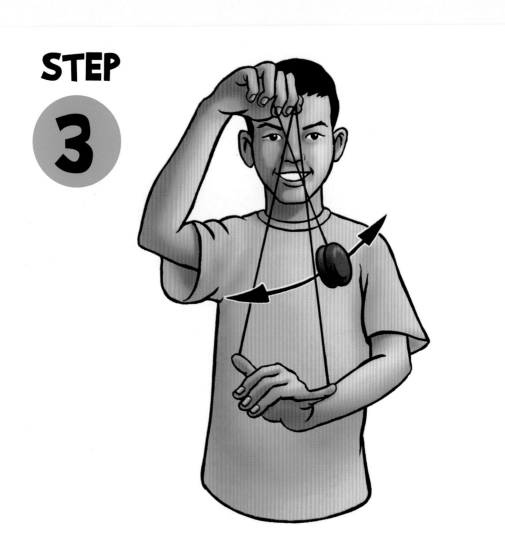

rock through it. Once you can do the cradle quickly without the yo-yo spinning you will be ready to do the trick with the Sleeper.

To end this trick drop the cradle string towards the ground. A quick jerk of the string will cause the yo-yo to return to your hand.

TIP: This trick will look better if your cradle is wide open at the bottom with the palm of your bottom hand facing down.

Loop The Loop

Let your yo-yo hang down at the end of its string. Turn the yo-yo several times to the right to tighten. The object of this trick is to throw the yo-yo forward and when it's on its way back to your hand, you push or flip the yo-yo forward again without catching it. After some practice, the goal is to do as many Loop the Loops as possible. As in Forward Pass, start Loop the Loop by preparing to throw the yo-yo forward. Start with your arm hanging down at your side. The back of your hand should be facing forward.

Take your arm back and then forward release the yo-yo just as your arm passes your hip with medium force. Aim your yo-yo straight ahead and extend your arm. When the yo-yo is returning and is six inches away from your hand, turn your wrist inward and push or flip the yo-yo forward again. It is important to do this motion with enough force. If done correctly the yo-yo will go forward and return to your hand time after time, allowing you to repeat the loops. To end this trick turn your palm facing forward and catch the yo-yo.

TIP: You will be able to do more loops if your string is very tight.

THE WORLD RECORD FOR
LOOP THE LOOP IS 21,663
IN THREE HOURS AND
ALMOST 9000 IN ONE HOUR.
FAST EDDY HOLDS BOTH RECORDS.

HOW MANY CAN YOU DO?

ADVANCED TRICKS

The Man On The Flying Trapeze

This is a difficult trick to master. I still remember the first time I did this trick and how excited I was to finally get it! It's an extension of the Breakaway trick. If you can't do the Breakaway perfectly, you won't be able to do this trick. This trick starts by bending your arm up at your side as if you're making a muscle. With your palm facing

STEP

2

out, throw your yo-yo in an outward casting motion causing the yo-yo to sleep. You need to use extra force when throwing the yo-yo for this trick. Now guide the yo-yo across your body using your lower arm and wrist as you would for Breakaway. Extend your index finger on your free hand and allow the string to flip around your index finger. Here is the tough part: the goal is to land the yo-yo so that the groove rests on top of the string. The index finger should be placed six inches from the yo-yo so that the yo-yo will land on the string easily. To end this trick drop the string and the yo-yo from your hands towards the ground. If the Sleeper is long enough, with a quick jerk the yo-yo will return to your hand.

TIP: When swinging the yo-yo over your index finger, the closer you can place the yo-yo to your finger, the better your chances of landing the yo-yo on the string. You can do it! It just takes hours of practice to learn.

Did you know...

...that the world's first yo-yo competition, won by 13-year-old Harvey Lowe, was held in London, England in 1932?

...that the largest yo-yo in the world weighs 256 pounds? Its string is 75 feet long and it really works!

...that the yo-yo has gone to space? It was taken aboard the shuttle Discovery on April 12, 1985.

...that Donald F. Duncan, whose company sold over 600 million yo-yos, introduced the looped yo-yo string, which allowed the Sleeper?

...that June 6 of every year is Yo-Yo Day?

...the clutch yo-yo was invented in 1980 by Michael Caffrey?

...the largest yo-yo competition in the world is the International Yo-Yo Open held every August in New York City?

step

1

The Monkey Climbing The Tree

This is a fun trick to do, and to watch! The objective of this trick is to have the yo-yo climb up the string and return to your hand. As with many tricks, this one starts with a long Sleeper—this one should be your longest. Take the index finger of your free hand and insert your index finger into the string from the back half way down the string. Bend the string over your index finger.

50

step

2

You can now insert the string into the yo-yo. If you pull down on the string the yo-yo will appear to climb up the string. When doing this trick do it at eye level. Also, tilt the string and the yo-yo towards you so that the yo-yo will sit on the string. When the yo-yo reaches the top of the string, remove your index finger from the top and the yo-yo will return to your hand.

TIP: Be sure you are putting the string into the yo-yo from the back, which is the side that is facing you.

The Brain Twister

This trick really will twist your brain while you're learning it, but with practice, you'll get it. Then you can twist other people's brains as they figure out how you do it!

step

2

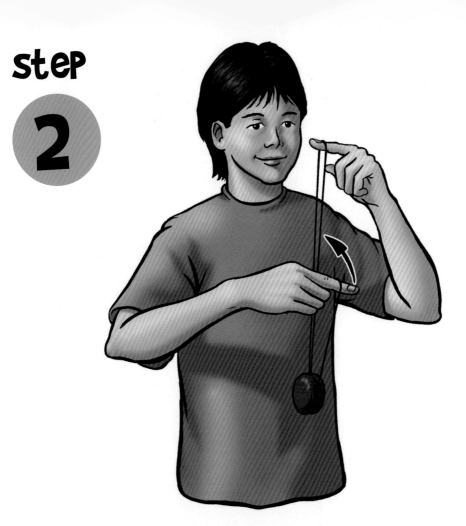

Begin by throwing a really long sleeper. Then, as you did for The
Monkey Climbing The Tree — take the index finger of your free hand
and place it against the string from the back half way down the
string. Bend the string over your index finger. Insert the string into
the yo-yo, and bring your yo-yo hand up under the yo-yo itself. Stick
the index finger of the hand holding the yo-yo, into the loop of string
you've just created.

step

3

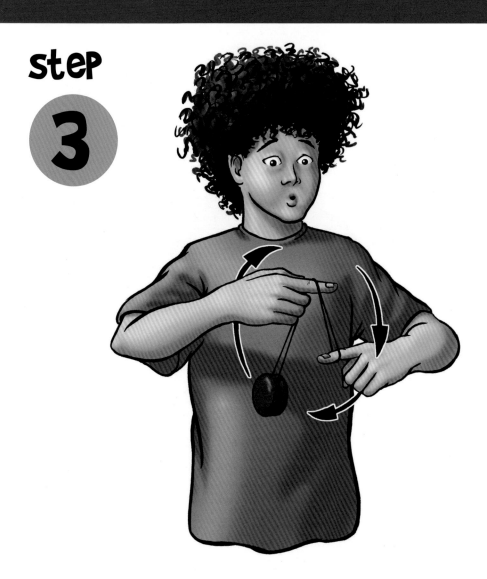

Flip the yo-yo out and away from your body, and spin it several times by using the hand not holding the yo-yo string as a sort of crank, pushing it away from your body.

step

4

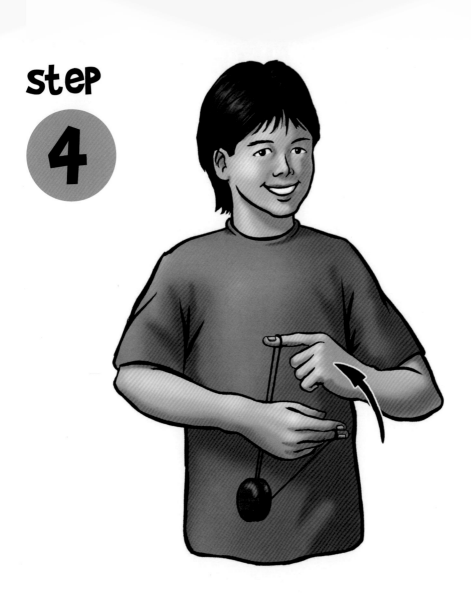

To finish the trick, reverse the direction of the spinning so that the yo-yo flips towards you. This should release it from the string and allow it to drop towards the ground. A flick of the wrist should wake the yo-yo up from its sleep and allow it to return to your hand.

ABOUT THE AUTHOR

"Fast" Eddy McDonald began his yo-yo career early, and by the age of 16 was touring the world, performing in more than 25 countries. After returning to Canada, Eddy solidified his status as a world champion by setting three Guinness World Records: most Loop The Loop in one hour (a staggering 8,437), most Loop The Loop in three hours (a mind-boggling 21,663), and most tricks in one minute where the yo-yo must return to the hand after each trick (35).

Fast Eddy has visited thousands of schools performing his amazing live yo-yo show and delivering his powerful message: "You can learn how to do almost anything with hard work and practice."

Fast Eddy continues to perform both nationally and internationally. He was born in Toronto, Canada.

Check him out online at: www.youtube.com/fasteddytalks